PETER LAFFERTY is a former secondary school science teacher. Since 1985 he has been a full-time author of science and technology books for children and family audiences, and has written over 50 books. He has contributed to and edited many scientific encyclopedias and dictionaries.

BETTY ROOT was the Director of the Reading and Language Information Centre at the University of Reading in England for over twenty years. She has worked on numerous children s books, both fiction and non-fiction.

SHIRLEY WILLIS was born in Glasgow, Scotland. She has worked as an illustrator, designer, and editor, mainly on books for children.

BOOK EDITOR: KAREN BARKER
TECHNICAL CONSULTANT: PETER LAFFERTY
LANGUAGE CONSULTANT: BETTY ROOT

AN SBC BOOK, CONCEIVED, EDITED AND DESIGNED BY THE SALARIYA BOOK COMPANY, 25, MARLBOROUGH PLACE, BRIGHTON, EAST SUSSEX BN1 1UB, UNITED KINGDOM.
' THE SALARIYA BOOK COMPANY LTD MCMXCVIII

FIRST AMERICAN EDITION 1998 BY FRANKLIN WATTS
GROLIER PUBLISHING CO., INC., 90 SHERMAN TURNPIKE, DANBURY, CT 06816

ISBN 0 531 11832 0 (LIB. BDG.)
ISBN 0 531 15982 5 (PBK.)

VISIT FRANKLIN WATTS ON THE INTERNET AT: HTTP://PUBLISHING.GROLIER.COM

Library of Congress Cataloging-in-Publication Data
Willis, Shirley.
  Tell me why rain is wet / Shirley Willis.
  p.   cm. — (Whiz kids) Includes index.
  Summary: Questions and answers explain water, the water cycle, and such aspects of weather as rain, clouds, ice, and snow. Includes experiments and activities.
  ISBN 0 531 11832 0
  1. Hydrologic cycle — Juvenile literature. 2. Weather — Juvenile literature. [1. Water — Miscellanea. 2. Hydrologic cycle — Miscellanea. 3. Weather — Miscellanea. 4. Questions and answers.]
I. Title. II. Series.   GB848.W55 1999
                551.48 — dc21   98-33553 CIP AC

GROLIER PUBLISHING

WHIZ KIDS

CONTENTS

Wherever you see
this sign, ask an
adult to help you.

WHIZ KIDS

TELL ME WHY RAIN IS WET

SPLASH!

SHIRLEY WILLIS

W

FRANKLIN WATTS
A Division of Grolier Publishing
NEW YORK • LONDON • HONG KONG • SYDNEY
DANBURY, CONNECTICUT

WHAT IS WATER?

Water has no color, taste, smell, or shape of its own.

It comes in three different forms: liquid, solid, and invisible gas.

Most of the water that we use every day is in its liquid form.

SPLOSH!

SPLASH!

Ice is water that has frozen and become solid because it is cold.

When water is heated it turns into an invisible gas called water vapor, or steam.

BBrrr!

7

WHO NEEDS WATER?

Every living thing needs water: all people, animals, and plants.

TWO-THIRDS OF YOUR BODY IS MADE UP OF WATER

When your body gets hot it sweats. Sweat is water that comes out of tiny holes in your skin called pores. This is how you cool off.

8

DOES WATER REALLY MAKE THINGS GROW?

You need: Mustard and cress seeds.
Two small plastic trays
lined with paper towels.

LEFT   RIGHT

1. Put a little water on the paper towel in the right-hand tray.
2. Scatter the seeds in both trays.
3. Put the trays near a window.
4. Each day add a little water to the right-hand tray to keep it damp.

Which seeds are growing?

The seeds in the right-hand tray are growing because water makes things grow.

ONIONS MAKE YOU CRY

Tears are made of water. When onions sting your eyes, tears help to wash them out.

PING!

SPLASH!

WHAT IS RAIN?

Rain is water
that falls from clouds.

CAN YOU MEASURE RAIN?

You need: A plastic bottle
Scissors
Measuring cup

1. Cut the top off the bottle. (Get an adult to help you with the scissors).
2. Turn the top upside down and push it into the bottle.
3. Stand the bottle in the garden. Make sure it is not close to any trees, as they will stop rain from falling into the bottle.

Each day measure the rain in the bottle using the measuring cup. Some days it will be empty.

1

2

3

WHAT ARE CLOUDS?

Clouds float in the sky.

Each cloud is made up of millions of tiny specks of water called water droplets.

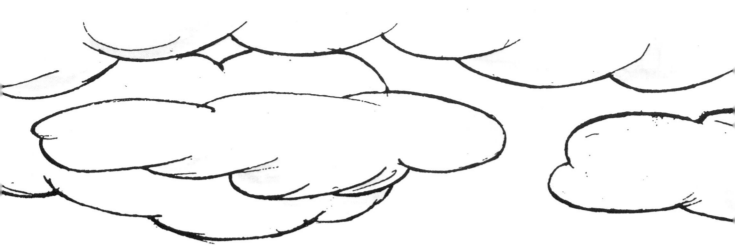

The water droplets are so light that they float in the air.

THERE ARE THREE MAIN TYPES of CLOUDS

<u>Cumulus</u> clouds are fluffy.

<u>Stratus</u> clouds are flat.

<u>Cirrus</u> clouds are thin and wispy.

PUDDLES SEEM TO SHRINK!

WHERE DO PUDDLES GO?

Heat from the sun turns some of the water from the ground and the sea into water vapor.

14

Water vapor is an invisible gas that rises into the air when water is warm.

When water turns into water vapor it is called evaporation.

WATCH THAT PUDDLE

After it rains, draw a chalk line around a puddle. The puddle will get smaller and smaller until it disappears. Some of the water soaks into the ground but the rest evaporates.

IT'S EVAPORATED!

15

HOW ARE CLOUDS MADE?

Water vapor keeps rising into
the air until it cools down again.

When water vapor lands on dust,
it forms water droplets.
This is called condensation.

The tiny water droplets
now float in the air and
form a cloud.

16

17

CAN YOU SEE CONDENSATION?

Steam is another name for water vapor.

When steam lands on a cold mirror, it cools down and turns back into water.

You can see condensed water on a steamy bathroom mirror.

18

WHY DOES RAIN FALL?

Inside a cloud the tiny water droplets keep moving and bumping together. With each bump they join up and get bigger.

This is how a raindrop is formed.

When sunlight shines through raindrops in the sky, sometimes it looks like the light is split into different colors. This is called a rainbow.

A single raindrop is made up of about one million tiny water droplets.

The colors in a rainbow are red, orange, yellow, green, blue, indigo, and violet.

As raindrops grow bigger, they get too heavy to float. Then they fall from the cloud as rain.

Blow some bubbles with soapy water. Now look at them closely. Can you see the colors of a rainbow?

21

WHY IS RAIN WET?

Rain is wet because it is water in its liquid form.

Rain sometimes falls as a light shower or as a fine drizzle.

22

A heavy rainfall makes everything wet very quickly.

SPLOSH!

23

WHAT IS ICE?

Ice is frozen water.
When it is very cold, water changes from a liquid form into a solid form called ice.

Icicles are formed when the air around us warms up and then quickly cools down again. As it gets warmer, snow and ice begin to melt and drip. But if it gets cold again, the drips freeze into long fingers of ice called icicles.

Water can be frozen into any shape. An ice cube left in the sun will melt and turn back into water. See how quickly its shape disappears.

MAKE YOUR OWN POPSICLES

You need: Fruit juice
Clean yogurt containers
Popsicle sticks

1

2

1. Pour some juice into each container, then put them in the freezer.

2. Take the Popsicles out of the freezer when partly frozen. Now push sticks into the middle of the containers.

Return the containers to the freezer until frozen.

WHAT IS SNOW?

If the air inside a cloud is very cold, the water droplets freeze and turn into ice crystals.

The ice crystals stick together to make a snowflake.

When snowflakes get too heavy, they fall from the clouds. Then it is snowing.

HOW TO MAKE A SNOWMAN

1. Make a snowball and roll it in the snow until it is big enough for a snowman s body.

2. Do the same again to make a smaller ball for his head.

3. Make his eyes and mouth with stones and his nose with a twig or a carrot.

WHAT GOES UP AND DOWN?

When water evaporates to form a cloud, it falls again as rain, hail, or snow. It then runs into the streams, rivers, and seas.

Now it evaporates all over again.

Water goes up but it always comes down again.

The never-ending journey of the earth's water is called the water cycle.

GLOSSARY

cloud   When tiny drops of water or ice group together and float in the sky.

condensation   When water vapor cools off and turns into a liquid.

drizzle   Very fine rain.

evaporation   When water is heated up slowly and turns into a gas.

hail   Balls of ice that are formed inside a cold storm cloud.

ice   Frozen water.

ice crystal   Water that has turned into tiny pieces of ice.

rain   Drops of water that fall from a cloud.

snow   Ice crystals that join together and fall as snowflakes from a cloud.

steam   Water vapor.

water   A liquid that has no color, smell, taste, or shape and is an important part of all living things.

water cycle   The never-ending movement of water as it rises from the seas to become clouds, falls as rain, and flows back into the seas.

water vapor   Water that has turned into a gas in the air.

INDEX